FANCY FASTWATER

FANCY
FASTWATER

ALBY BLAZO

Love, Luna Press

ISBN 978-7363534-1-7
Written by Alby Blazo
Front cover image by Megan Tenbusch

First Printing, 2021
Published by Love, Luna Press

Visit www.lovelunapress.com

Contents

ALWAYS FALL APART

CAPTIVE

WALLS OF HOME

LITTLE SPECKS

PARALLAX

For
my Luna, my Love

Melbourne

PAST DISPUTES

bullets of words
friendly fire is too kind
lodged shrapnel
cuts each vein
pours into teacups
sustenance in the trenches

A NOTE OF BLESSING
AND GOOD RIDDANCE

Who gave you the news?

I packed the past up into a single bag
stepped away in the night
there was no pause on the tarmac
no hopeful, backward glance
the window shade kept closed
no last image to engrave.

As the wheels folded in
I whispered,

so long, and thanks for nothing.

I WON'T SEE YOU IN MELBOURNE

the streets are full of your absence
head never turning to check the shadows
chocked with graffiti and coffee mugs

the trams scream of arrival
always coming, always greeting
only the betrayal of minutes, nothing more

you will not find me in the alleys
or Victoria Market
or on the Williamstown line

this is the land of freedom
land of opportunity
because you are not here

FOLDED BY WEATHER

storm clouds gather over the sofa
tornado winds buffet the dining room
tsunami rains brew in the bath
like an umbrella
I fold

SHE IS GONE, SHE IS SCARED

upon unpacking
hands ached
to repack each item
to hold plane tickets

instead they pulled
blankets close
tuned out the clock
slept for too long

held my heart up

THE POET AND THE ARTIST

too many layers
metaphors and paint
undiscovered topography

mountains of paper
stories and sketches
sorting through us

brush our history
to the floor,
come to bed

rediscover hillsides
clavicles and knees
remove the layers

ABBOTSFORD

the train out of town
leaving a taste
for a breath
past empty buildings
over sidewalk cracks
kalaidoscoping the
last place we spoke
as your fingers slipped
from mine

NO NAME

settled in my chest
curled through each rib
an unseen corset

shuddering lungs
begging for breath
and easy movement

peek between layers of skin
crack my bones
search my marrow

weighing me down
without the courtesy
of signing your work

Unnamed Inches

ABOVE, ALL

at the head of the table
cut the meat small
nibble vegetables
forks on plates
a chair whispers, coughs
it's too much
you escape
to fill the bird feeder

POWERLESS, ALWAYS

moon stuck on full
tide not ebbing
wind bashing
words against skin
hiding ink beneath sleeves
kitchen knife too dull
call up the dark

There, Listen 1

EINS

unmasked eyes
descry Daedalus's walls
sheath your arrow
I am still here
we both know
I'm not destined to be
among the stars

ZWEI

Pull the blinds
the light lies,
too orange
too bright.
Unnaturally near,
the porch light
shines,
overpowering
my moon.

DREI

I slept under your watch
now I lay restless
no longer reveling in your rays

I open the window
a false light fills the pane
merely the orange glow
of a neighbor's lamp

VIER

On the nights the moon is gone
I cannot sleep.

You steal across the road,
knock on the neighbor's door
and ask them to turn on their porch light.

Approximately 3.2km Deep in the Rhein Between Wiesbaden and Mainz

SUCH LARGE PALMS

fingers barely reaching
the edge of your palms
wanted mine to match,
to mimic the breadth and lines —
places I couldn't follow —
a split line and wrinkles
paths to places
you'll never see

WHISPERED THE QUEEN TO THE WATER

running along the river
she never stepped far
promises of rapids and falls
no voices in the rocks
waiting to slip,
hidden from the tempest

hold me, she whispered

OLD WINDS IN NEW FAMILIES

table laden with voices
vases of smiles and teeth
songs of laughter

my chair is a teacup
winds whisper
screams of lullabies
bowls of grimaces and tongues
feasts of mothers

storm unnoticed
I fold my hands
erode my face —
wait to be alone

BRIGHT AND SHINY

split ends
half-clean hair
sweater misbuttoned
lunch spilling out
I arrive late
phone still at home

later, I'll ask the stars
to make me more like them,
bright and shiny

STAND UP, NEVER FALL AGAIN

years behind the bathroom door
cowering against the mirror
begging to be let through

when the door broke
I stabbed your heart
beating in my wrists

stepping over your body
I have a crowbar spine
cactuses for hands

my heart sits with wet towels
on the bathroom floor —
no longer needed

LIGHT A CANDLE

the bed is empty on your side
the darkness heavier than the duvet,
I rise to light a candle
placed in the window
calling you home

only the moths knock,
asking me to fly

I would fly to you

FINAL EULOGY FOR BARREN HANDS

when there are no pens
and my wrists ache
unable to hold out my hands
to offer up myself
to strangers and you
I will cross the grave
in a January frost
unmarked stone mirrors me
nothing to say

THE HOME MAKERS

perchance the smile, unbroken teeth,
piano scales of laughter
a knowing walk
I pick at them
try them on in the mirror
nothing fits
sofa too deep
frameless walls
house, not home

ANNA BETH

she hunches in the corner
drawing eraser pictures
dragons and dinosaurs
never still,
can't look them in the eye
Anna Beth doesn't pay attention
she was told that she was smart
she can be anything she wants —
but she never wants

she no longer believes them
doesn't understand how,
how she can be important,
when she can't even manage happy

her arms overreach the table
wrists peeking out
evidence of her difference
unable to hide the flash,
the carved map of her body
red shooting stars and milky way

her arms were meant
for reaching across distances
places beyond her classroom

but a child seeks normality
and she forgot
that she could be an airplane,
contenting herself with a cello
the only time it was okay
to reach in upon herself
join with the instrument
hide within the strings
until anyone could play her

and they play her so well
into corners and therapy,
never satisfied with her sound
so she slices off more
carving out their instrument
so maybe one day
they will be happy

HOWEVER, PERHAPS I WAS WRONG

no one said, Don't go

determined to travel
searching for home
along rivers and cliffs,
beneath ravens and parrots
pecking away
until nothing's left

but no one said, Don't go

JOYOUS SHOUTS FOR INNOCENT CORPSES

childhood teams
fraction
seek new allies
breed spies
baptized in faith
of family feuds

FIRST FOUND LAND

sliding doors
I roll forward
overpacked
he takes me in-hand
managing my baggage
stranger danger,
but I follow
lighter now
new place, new rules

EVERYONE, INCLUDING THE RIVER

head down, slide through
nothing fast, nothing worth noting
stay dark, hug the current

dam growing
shoring up poisons
a mousy façade

never not noticed
enough to get by —
to appear clean

There, Listen 2

FÜNF

You grow fat
on my secrets
as I lie awake,
whispering release.
Until you're thin
again.
Where did they go?
Who did you tell?
I'm losing all trust,
with your coming
and going.

SECHS

How many nights
have I lain awake
ready to join
the hunt?
But she never asks.

Artemis,
let me atone,
draw a bow.
I shall lay the stag
at your feet,
content among
my sisters.

SIEBEN

My body is predominantly
water.
Is there any wonder then,
that you pull my heart —
strings so?

ACHT

There is nowhere
I can go
to hide from you.
Your light
always
finds me.

Spring Excursion

IT WAS THE DAY AFTER EASTER

words form stories
in the air
egg hunts and ham
family gathering galore

over my shoulder,
my empty house
with vacant chairs
microwave meals and tv

LAST RAINFALL IN NOISY G.R.

baking trays and plates
precariously tower,
waiting to spill
into boxes

cloud tears
soak the truck bed,
every possession I own —
sirens speed past, calling farewell

There, Listen 3

NEUN

you chase your love
across the heavens
never catching up —
told you're merely
a reflection
yet you spill your light
so generously
across the water

ZEHN

You are more
than your brother's
reflection.
You hold the reins
of night.
Give the command,
and we'll hunt him
like a stag.

ELF

You surrendered
to the thread of Ariadne
and Gleipnir,
asked nothing in return
for your brother's protection.
Yet he still runs
from you.

ZWÖLF

they name the darkness
New Moon —
I call it yet another,
Abandonment

DREIZEHN

Don't let me be buried
beneath the soil.
Lay me out on Gaia.
Let Artemis be
my lantern
for eternity.

Feeling for a Heartbeat/The Value of Land

I DON'T FEEL

strong, you say

familial names never cross my lips
silence reigns, coating my skin
a ghost, treading lightly
there will be no trace

heartless, she says

WHY I'M NOT AFRAID

like before
I saw ahead
no fortune-teller needed,
I accepted with
daffodil spine and steel eyes
trodden forward,
held my own hand

harder to live through
even knowing it was coming

Always Fall Apart

FRIDAY NIGHT, AT A PARTY

collage of faces
half-remembered dream
everyone's here,
I know no one
broken record stories
compete with smoke,
wander room to room

red solo empty
nothing but foam

FIRST ODE FOR RED HEARTS

I've painted daffodils
to hang on each wall,
brought the sun inside

I've fluffed each pillow
the settee ready
china placed

there is a room in my heart
dedicated to you

Captive

THE ARRIVAL

I made the choice,
sacrificed a dream for a dream
Auntie for Scholar
ribcage constricted
feet unfettered

until my breath arrived
releasing your name
naming me anew —
Godmother

SOFTER DISCORDS

lying awake in silence,
wait for the lullaby
that never comes
I replay the notes in my mind,
soft voices
rising with the moon
light of an abandoning car
traversing the ceiling
prison bars of blinds
night brings the softer sounds —
harsh in the dawn

ST. STEPHAN KIRCHE MELODIES

subtle crescendos
of plums splashing

no staccato steps
on stones worn down

only me and warm wood
overly wrought and settled

surrounded in faded light
of swirling bruises

Chagall's blues blossoming
beneath my skin

REWRITE THIS PLACE

move our buildings closer
let's walk from one to the other
so our feet never leave the ground
paint peony blushes on the buildings
and ivy mascara on the windows
we'll tattoo our shadows on the brick
and carve our prayers on the corners
mumbling our steps into the sidewalks

let's rewrite our city in our name

THE NOTE

silence deafening in the aftermath,
left alone with argumentative ghosts
I pull on shorts, perhaps a jacket
step into the snow
let it swirl my agitated heart
make my way to the river
sit where there used to be trees
admire the surface that used to be rapid
the color that used to be clean
sail a paper boat
the note drifts on, pulled under

I'm letting go, let me go

DANGER IN THE TREES/LAMENT
FOR MICHIGAN

I wrote down each reason I loved you
posted them on the trees
you cut them down
sent them down river
unlit pyres,
the ones unfit for Baker
left to wither with disease

yet I came back
send me back

THE LEAST SINFUL DANDELION

I avoid the cracks
slip off to the side
barely taking any light
keep myself small
hoping to stay unnoticed,
hoping to stay alive

still,
you find me
again and again,
cutting me down
digging at my roots
until my petals
lay torn

but
at least I remain
colorful

A RUNE

I write your name
carving each letter
the pieces you hide,
never naming the shadows
I draw them out
shaping the secrets
that build your spine
I wrap each letter
of mine around
each of yours,
creating a language of us

RIVERSIDE PARK

slow walk
along the flat water
where we bury our dead

benches litter the path
places to stoop
crumble into tears
spill them out onto the pavement
let them tumble to the river
creating rapids of our own

YOUR NAME, COUNTLESS TIMES

I cry your name out
to the dark sky
beg for help
knees to earth
scream please
over and over

my cracked voice
echoes back
your name
over and over
again

NOTHING SEEN

breakfast table avoided
nothing seen

lunch table empty
nothing seen

dinner table sparse
nothing seen

A SOLID VESSEL

you saw me break
watched from a distance
didn't even sweep me up,
I crawled back into myself
glued my joints
rigidly upright

I'll never stoop
to scrape you into
a dustpan
when the time comes

OUR HEALTHY CORPSES
AND THE ORGAN GROWS

sit us in rows
weight our heads
against our hands
clasped in beggary
as the organ takes over
swells the pipes
heating hearts long cold

raise us with notes
carry us in melodies
let us abandon
these skins and bones

US APART

You came to visit
crossed the ocean
told me your story
but nothing is
different.
You can go home
now.

Walls of Home

LOWELL, MI 1943

the baseball uniform
stood out on Main Street
as she walked past

he stood in the doorway
of the bowling alley
noted her stride

he fulfilled his pledge
taking vows and her to wife

with matching steps
they went home

LAST LOOK BEFORE LETTING GO

as it's always been
covered in ice
white on white
idealized dream
when it's just cold
I meant to say goodbye
but couldn't slow the car,
skidded by, slipping past
as we should have done
from the beginning
no turning back
everything's ice now

GIRL (IN PICTURE)

nothing is written
on the back
no clues to the date
or even location
something familiar
flickers in the eyes
the curve of her hand
frozen with an almost
smile, uncertain

I want to shout
stop, not one step more
but she won't listen
I never have
and now I'm left unnamed,
in this photograph

IMAGES FROM HOUSES 1988-2010

heads bent close
bodies huddled
flatline smiles
empty eyes

in the corner
curved over
a book
I sit

TO THE MARQUISE OF ABANDONMONT

taught each
flick of the tongue
swish of the fist

I'll descend
the staircase
keep my hands
to myself
pick up my hem
and run

sunny window patch
stretches through the book
solitary peacefulness
surrounded by familial afterthoughts
the newspaper, a gauntlet thrown

Oxford — Tudor Seminar

they fall away with the seasons
window's light remains
stepping through blinds
touching down among lakes
to become a Romantic

LEAVE SAD HERE

empty the shelves
check behind crockery
strip the walls of art
wrap each memory
in clean tissues
placing them in boxes
tied with twine
stack the tchotchkes,
the creaking aches
beneath the web awning
and leave memory lane behind

THE FAMILY WE ABANDONED 1999

it ended with a phone call
wrapped in plaid
it ended with a lie
or a misplaced memory

snow still fell
blanketing your face
pretending innocence
feigning heartbreak

no more phone calls
one less chair
no more plaid
one less family

MAN (TALKING)

tell me again to smile
to put my best foot forward
Daddy knows best

explain, just one more time
how I'll change my mind
chase motherhood

lecture on the grammatical
differences I won't comprehend
en-dashes and em-dashes

talk loud enough
I can dash away
and you'll never notice

ORDINARY MEALTIME

the door is locked
there are no lights on
my shoes the only pair
on the rug by the door
I wash my lunch dish
pull leftovers from the fridge
don't bother with the oven
or the cookware
only the microwave
I sit on the sofa
tv for conversation
no words from my lips
I wash the plate alone
I fall asleep alone

COSMOLOGICAL ITEMS
[OBJECTS IN SPACE]

let me journey
past the ether and planets
the moons and stars
to settle among the Oort
still revolving around you
but I need the space
the cloud of my rings
turmoiled and grey
I could settle for a comet
visiting for a moment
rocketing past

but we both know
I burn for you

Little Specks

ALPHA

The view is clear
yet I wish for leaves
to cover dying stalks.
Is this what lies ahead,
death and destruction?
Even the trees cry out,
for they have seen the road.

BETA

track each hoof mark
place my steps in his,
down the banks of the river
Thanatos rides on,
I've forgotten to follow

GAMMA

There is a reason
Persephone
is my favorite
myth.
Hades,
come
collect me.

DELTA

The dead don't speak,
nor do we.
My name will fade.
The dead disappear.

EPSILON

the banshee cries,
I learn to wail
and embroider my
still-beating heart —
too many strings,
not enough poppies

ZETA

we'll rust
in the rain
seek shelter
from flesh
cast ourselves
with wood

free the flame

ETA

Each morning
I pull out the ruler,
measure one hair at a time,
the millimeters since you've gone.
How many inches until I'm steady?
Three? Four?
Ten inches and still my fingers shake.
You kept yours short
framed your face with mourning,
sheared swaths of possibilities.
Each morning
I reach for the scissors
unable to pick them up
to cut your absence into my reflection.

AN ARRIVAL — LIVE

step off the plane
home again
no welcome
empty house
walk to the gas station
pick up a sandwich
make plans for dinner
meals cancelled
sit alone in the basement
leave again,
ready to feel whole
in a foreign place

Parallax

AMBER STONE

The necklace,
given to a child,
quickly misplaced.
The dragon fly
wings outspread
but encased,
long dead —
still forced
to be beautiful.

ROBINSON ROAD ONE

In childhood
twenty minutes
is closer to an hour,
a journey
to the cold house
inhabited by a cold family.
A wall of windows
separated nature
a place to look, but
never touch,
a family motto.

If only they really had been,
a full hour away
or more.

ROBINSON ROAD TWO

I race the whole way
from where I lived
to where I live
among students, strangers

an involved introvert
more than content
among the ghosts

CHAMOMILE AND EXHAUSTION

One more.
A broken record,
the only words
I whisper
with any strength.
I crawl beneath
sheets too fresh
to hold you.
Folded under the waves,
my lips release
your name,
a dying day wish.

A NOT SO CUTE PANIC

No more.
No more phone calls
or letters stuffed in mailboxes
not even the ones
written by another hand.
They go straight
into the incinerator
my heart was thrown into
years ago.

NORTH OF MICHIGAN

lungs
no longer ironclad
soft and full,
ribs removed
left behind in the rapids,
I don't need
anything to protect
my heart here
I'll introduce myself
instead
by my name

GLANCE FROM MY PORCH STEP

when it's time to rest
prop up tired feet
spare a glance
to the road where the sun sets

I could follow the light
let it lead me on
past the post office
and highways

perhaps the next time
the sun leaves,
I'll join

STEPFALLS BY THE CREEK

tie-rails
de-knobbed doors
shallow waters
but we don't touch
cross to the burning barrel
contribute photos
small mementos
we don't want to remember,
don't want to cross again
to the other side
the country side

WHERE ARE YOU

(UNDISCLOSED LOCATION)

there are rules
to living life on the lam
methods of over-the-shoulder peeks
a specific style of hat (with a brim)
carry no treasure
beyond the plane ticket
in your pocket,
admit to no past
you've only just begun
and when asked where you're going —
only forward

ME WANING

moon and sun
circle in tandem
forever giving chase

I am not the moon
you are no sun

let me instead sit
beneath a tree
listen to stories on the wind

I will never seek you
nor seek to be sought

Alby Blazo is best known for short myths and even shorter poems. She's published in several anthologies and is part of multiple international writers groups. Alby can often be found out in the garden or admiring her cat.

CPSIA information can be obtained
at www.ICGtesting.com
Printed in the USA
BVHW041737220322
632089BV00011B/1470